73

*Bring Down the Chandeliers*
a collection of poetry

℃ℬ

by Tara Hardy

Write Bloody Publishing
*America's Independent Press*

Long Beach, CA

WRITEBLOODY.COM

Hardy, Tara.
1ˢᵗ edition.
ISBN: 978-1-935904-30-4

Interior Layout by Lea C. Deschenes
Cover Designed by Joshua Grieve
Author Photo by Martin Horn
Cover Illustration by Lily Lin
Proofread by Jennifer Roach and Sarah Kay
Edited by Jamie Garbacik, Courtney Olsen, Alexis Davis, Sarah Kay, and Derrick Brown
Type set in Bergamo from www.theleagueofmoveabletype.com

Special thanks to Lightning Bolt Donor, Weston Renoud

Printed in Tennessee, USA

Write Bloody Publishing
Long Beach, CA
Support Independent Presses
writebloody.com

To contact the author, send an email to writebloody@gmail.com

*For Lily*

*BRING DOWN THE CHANDELIERS*

# BRING DOWN THE CHANDELIERS

Hummingbird ....................................................... 15

Daughter ............................................................... 16

Adam's Rib ........................................................... 18

Cigarette Lighter ................................................. 20

Octave .................................................................. 22

Sand ...................................................................... 23

Original Name ..................................................... 26

So Neutered ......................................................... 28

Hunger .................................................................. 30

Lizzie Borden ....................................................... 32

Homosexual Love ................................................ 34

Advice to a Trauma Survivor ............................. 35

Time ...................................................................... 38

Rules of Having a Mistress ................................. 39

Pussy Christ .......................................................... 40

Green Onions ....................................................... 41

Gin ........................................................................ 42

Widow ................................................................... 43

Outside My Face .................................................. 45

Your Missing ........................................................ 46

Hey, World ........................................................... 48

Sex from the Perspective of My Hair ................................................ 49

Her Own Road ................................................................................. 50

Fuck Christmas ................................................................................ 51

Rain Saws At .................................................................................... 52

Too Early .......................................................................................... 54

Advice to Anyone Loving a Trauma Survivor ............................... 55

Crow Funeral ................................................................................... 56

A Femme Is ...................................................................................... 57

The Day I Accidentally Caused the Death of a Baby Sunfish
and My Mother Called Me a Murderer ........................................... 59

Mental Illness .................................................................................. 60

String ............................................................................................... 62

Welcome Here .................................................................................. 63

Crayfish ............................................................................................ 64

Regret ............................................................................................... 66

Mistress ............................................................................................ 67

Along the Fault Line ........................................................................ 68

Your Throat ...................................................................................... 69

Parrot in a Pear Tree ....................................................................... 70

Uncommon Woman .......................................................................... 71

Eventuallys ....................................................................................... 73

Dandelions ....................................................................................... 74

Mother's Day .................................................................................... 76

Peace and Justice .......................................................................... 78

Life Story ...................................................................................... 80

About the Author ........................................................................... 83

Acknowledgments .......................................................................... 85

# HUMMINGBIRD

In the orphanage of my voice box
    my father sits, fork and knife upright
on the table before him. He's already cut

off my hummingbird and fed it
    to our dog. Scientists can't pin down
how hummingbirds are able to maintain

flight-flap at a pace so feverish when
    energy expelled exceeds energy consumed.
In place of my hummingbird my father

drapes a bib, so he won't have to look at his
    handiwork. But behind the curtain
the nurse explains in some sort of

capacity retained exceeds capacity consumed
    miracle I still have apparatus necessary
for flight. In an under the table deal of my

own I make faithful our dog, stroke the beast
    hold to his nose the scent of his master.
Make a bid as mistress to tear limb from

limb the obstruction of my father on the runway
    called my mouth, on the runway
called my other mouth. Itself an overcrowded

with cornered voices orphanage. As our hound
    hones his scent, all the children I ever
wasn't but was meant to be,

break open the roof, take wing,
        and I speak
            speak.

# DAUGHTER

What I want you to know is this:

> My father did monster things to my child body.
> This is a lamb's truth.

Like pouring bleach over grass he burned his name into me.
What he took no one can repay.

> Say this is a tax collector's truth,
> but also say this:

It did not make him powerful or grand.
He isn't somewhere cackling on a distant hill.

> He is at home, sleeping in a wool cap
> on a sinking sofa because he snores
> like the train that orphaned him at seven.
> He is an old man with a garden, pinching
> tomato bugs between thumb and forefinger.

You can say he is a doddering letch, but also say this:
Say he did the dishes, cooked; taught me how to fish.

> There is a boat still floating at the wharf
> from 1917, the same year he poked his
> puckered head through his mother's legs,
> squinting. The boat's rhythm against
> the water is his wet lungs still pulling
> breath. This is an organ's truth.

And me, say I am half of him, his monster flesh.
Pulled from his injury on my mother like a fist.

> Say I am a fist. I am not
> the pasty faces of incest children
> growing on the underbelly of a log,
> color of the way-inside of lettuce.

I am spunneling, alive, and red. This is an artery's truth.

> You can say I am half-blooded monster,
> but also say this: my
> blood does not make a pity trip.

The fist of me unfolds to pluck the quill of him from my throat and regularly fill it. This is a pen's truth.

> Six years ago, crossing his state's line
> caused my body to clutch itself so completely
> I couldn't pee for three days.
> Except in a long thin terrified stream.

A scream as long would have melted the road. The sticky tar of it.

> Say he stole from me the right
> to be around to bury him,
> but also say this:

I am not the road of tar. I was only stuck to it.
A wingless, but determined beast.

> This is a daughter's truth.

# ADAM'S RIB

*When a man I love hit a woman I love,*
*what I wish I'd said, but didn't:*

Inside Adam's rib is a kitchen. A yellow
kitchen. Inside Adam's rib is a container
of bees. Of scars. Of chases.

Inside Adam's rib is a wish. A woman

is a wish. For something more than salt
on your tongue. A woman is a wish
for something to puncture lonely.

A woman is a balm. Inside Adam's rib
is a remedy. A resurrection.
A spontaneous eruption

of wings. All of our possibilities
peeking skull-out from between the legs
of God. A rib is not a sword, Adam.

Do not use her as such. A rib
is not a mold. Do not expect her
to keep your form. A rib is but a strip

of marrow, a strip of life
upon which other life grows.
She is greenhouse. She is home

to paintbrush. Do not twist
it out of her hand. Do not ask her to take
back her glow. She is not in charge

of the moon, though the moon doth
forget himself. He thinks woman pulls
on him. It's why he reveals and

retracts his story one month at a time.
Yes, she will pull on your bones
bring their dust to your mouth, say

*breathe out,*
            scatter yourself. You are larger

than you behave, Adam.
Woman is not something to worry
in your pocket like a coin. She is

her own set of ribs, something to encase
a tide. Close your eyes, listen
to the waves. They speak

of your mother who, yes, did bend
at the hand of your father but came up
no less flower. A woman is not wilt,

she is a stalk. If she has to, she will root
in spoiled water. So, why would you feed her
anything less than wingbeat?

She doesn't want to hear I'm sorry.

She wants to hear the bees in your chest
making love. She knows of what
you are made. It is not fist or thrust.

It is woman. You are made of woman,
as much as she is made of Adam.
Adam, give her your knee,

the one on loan from God. Fill it
like a teacup with honey, offer it to
your resurrection in the kitchen.

# Cigarette Lighter

This is for the woman who makes your blood
run siren cold. Wrapped in flashing lights
her ear-shattering call causing your husband

to back out of the driveway. This is for her
pelvis, unnaturally flared. Early. Like a runway
for bees. She was never a calla lily, always

a moonflower. This is for being able to see
the reach of her reflection across the still
water of his night breath. The way his shoulder,

when he's near you, tucks in on itself like a lapel
with her name written underneath. Even when
he's not wearing a shirt. Especially when he's naked

does all his mammalian fuzz, the invisible hairs
on his chest, belly, the ones you've run your chin down
too many times to count, those tiny translucent arms

wave like underwater fronds to the rhythm of
her swish. Across town her forked tail shimmering
under her nightgown. When she sleeps, her breath

tastes of salted caramel, whole fruit syrups, and
his cum. This is for her. The one whose fingernails
you wake up with in your back as you swim in her

eye, the searchlight she's fixed on your house. Go
ahead, step out from behind your apron. Try to
get your breasts to dance like anything but prunes.

Entice him with a shave or grow out
in the place where he so greedily used to bathe
his face. But don't count the streetlights

under which she waits, or the number of times he
checks his email behind public restroom stalls.
Go ahead, put a candle under your mattress,

but don't expect the mine of your worth to cough
up anything but coal. Hell, go ahead and burn
down the house. Set the edges of your life

to the color of the cigarette lighter
you threatened to hold to your face the last time
he backed out of the driveway.

# Octave

Mama, I did not see him
untie you in the night,
your hem the pulling
of a string at the top
of a full feed sack. I did not
see the thick stem
of his index finger break
your seal, or the way
his hair, slick, stuck
to his forehead. I did
not see him put me
in your eye before
he put me in the middle
of the road called your
future. I could not
possibly have seen
his gold molar reflect
the lantern light.
But I did feel
the wheel of your wagon
break against my infant
spine. I heard the mama
cow mourn. Her
low moan land-whale grief
match octave with what
you should have shrieked.

# SAND

*If the sand could speak she might say:*

I am the sand. When people climb me, they
think I am a mountain, but I am one grain
at a time. Under me is sludge. Under me
are mollusks, the water table,

people's old rings, abandoned shoes,
driftwood that isn't drifting
anymore, under me is a nation of rust,
        under me is oil.

Some things I can contain: they are coughed
up uncontainable grief, but I contain
it. Here under my surface is an ocean
of widows, of orphans, open mouthed

cradles crying for their contents. Some
things I wish I could not contain: bones.
I am not the color I was meant to be,
have not the hue God gave me.

I am the color of an entire people's
humiliation, occupation, desecration.
        I am the color of a blood
red dawn. Something itself I wish

did not rise over me, did not push me
out of the dark to look at myself.
For I cannot be washed. Monsoons
pummel me, seas seep through me.

All I can do is fill my pockets
while always in my interstitial tissue
is the residue of death. I am the sand.
The very ground beneath the soldier's boot,

but I do not get a vote. I don't mind
being pissed on, or dug into to hold their shit.
        I don't mind their semen,
their snot, their spat out cores of lychee fruit,

old peels, wads of gum, even the butts
of their cigarettes. But when they rest
their guns on me, I wish I could open my mouth
and swallow. Instead I become

accomplice to murder. I carry their tanks,
their fates, their patriots, their false
        Gods. I carry their hopes
of being heroes, wrapped in the uniforms

of peer pressure. The reason men kill
other men: they don't want to look like pussies.
They spill their intestines, their livers,
their bladders, their throats, over my scape

so they don't have to be embarrassed.
If you ask an American of what he's most afraid,
he'll say being laughed at. If you ask an Iraqi
of what she's most afraid she'll say being killed.

        I carry their kill. Corpses. Open-mouthed

maggoted throats over my back on the way
to burial. In some nations
I am not much more than an only partially closed
mass grave. But I was meant to be something else.

I was meant to be the site of conception
under stars, of confession of want
to be taken in – sex as prayer not ethnic cleansing.
I am the sand. I do not have organ or heart,

but I can contain. Bring me your war—
split open my mouth and make me
wolf; I'll let the sea seep through me until
its machine is nothing but rust. I promise

to need more than your vote. So, remind you
the host of your body contains everything human
ever done. From torture to martyr, murder
to mother: Judas, Pharaoh, Abu Jahl. Noah,

Moses, Muhammad. I am but a reflection of you. The heat
from your feet forges me, mirror. So bring me
your best sweat. Bring me grace, mercy,
                absolution. Drive, oath, restitution.

Bring me your last, first, yet to be born daughter
and son. No blood but that of your birth, bring me
a movement one grain at a time. So, one day
in my name, world, we will reconcile with dawn.

# Original Name

Pompadour. Lullaby.
Words that mean something beyond
the something they mean:

Cradle is something I make with my back. Back
is something you build with wood,
scrap. Man is something you make

with your hands. Girl is someone I meet
in your church, the one you make
of my hips. We are not wanting

here. If only because here we are
only wanting. Our mouths don't get left
at the door with our shoes. Here, we are always

kicking to the surface like greedy trout. At dusk.
It is always dusk here. It clarifies our outlines.
On your jaw is your original name. The one

we came here to redeem. In my ears the breaking
of a bough when you push up. When you become
steeple to my confession. Confession is the thing

food is made of. Something to nourish. Something
to chew. Instead of our tongues. That we silence
in order to speak. Except when we speak in coins—

cursings thrown into fountains. Make sure they slap.
Make sure they pierce. Make sure they're cock-
sure. My third favorite word is pussy

but only when it's between your teeth. About to be spat
in my ear. Say barrel say bushel say something
to catch the rain. Which is sure to come. Come,

let us bend the bones of our necks to drink
the fall from the rain. To drink the night
from the moon. Bowl me down with it.

Catch yourself in the man in it. We are only
ever rocks. Borrowed from his mirrored hands.
So, all there is to do is wind one up

and pitch. Listen, Pompadour,
something is making the track rumble.
I think it's a fucking lullaby.

# SO NEUTERED

To everyone else, so neutered due to his age and oddity; he was mostly a penis to me. The kids at the bus stop used to ask in a searingly hissed voice, "Is *that* your father?" It was always the *that* that slapped me the hardest. Hardened my nipples with shame. I only ever learned how weird he was to everyone else when I had to put shoes on and go to school.

No one has ever caused me to form around a scar more profoundly, but every single day I tasted the bitter ear wax of pity for him when I got off the bus. Found him tenderly pinching potato bugs off his babies in the garden. At dinner, his thumb and forefinger would be tea-stained with their sacrifice. We ate fresh vegetables for months from his loving attention to what grew in the ground. He was always good with a spade. Taught me to plant marigolds to keep the rabbits out.

Sometimes I went willingly between the walls of the garages to "help him out." Not because I feared him, but because I felt sorry for him. None of the other kids would have ever willingly called him daddy, put warm red socks smelling of peppermint in his Christmas stocking. I wanted to want him as my father. But I also wanted to hide him. Didn't want his tea stain on me. To carry his oddity into my life, what began with that first dirty sneaker step onto the rubber floored bus, which always smelled like Lysol, someone's fried breakfast trapped on their clothes, and freedom.

I studied hard. One hundred percent on every page meant someday I could maybe buy him the right pants and collared shirts to fit in and make a friend. He only ever had one. My whole life. Imagine a man with only one friend for forty years of his adult life. Imagine his intimacy with the soil. And the dog, before he killed her. Imagine the sweet stink of onions right out of the garden on his breath on your kindergarten forehead. Imagine the A's you're stacking like ladders. The potato bug of pity that thrives in your belly every time he walks you to the bus.

Imagine being willing to give back half of where those A's have taken you if it would buy him a marigold plot of friends. If only because their kindness to him might neuter your childhood night.

# HUNGER

Hunger is but an indication I'm alive.
Also, a way to stay numb. Sober,
I can't afford anesthesia, so I starve
myself on purpose, float
through my day on partial
disconnect. Hunger is but a way
to have power. She said,
"You're not pretty, but the women
in this family have always been
thin." Thin is power. Hunger is
but a way to keep razors from
my wrists. The slow secret
way I can harm myself while
looking victorious to my friends.
Hunger is a way to say I'm better
than them. They may be younger,
smarter, prettier, but I know how to win
the race to thin, to skin and bones, to
skeleton. No matter that my hair falls
out in the shower, my lips are always
chapped and everyone can hear my
stomach begging me to let myself
out of this pen. Embarrassed and
superior is an interesting cocktail
to bring to any affair. Hunger is
a way to show myself that I'm not
worthy of basic human desires.
Food as need is debatable at this
point. Hunger is a way to get over
him. Crying down the highway
I throw food out the window. At work,
I flush a candy bar down the toilet
so I won't eat it. At home, I tell myself
how pretty the cupboard looks with
everything sealed. Don't break the seal.
When people come over they won't

say I don't have food, but sealed is safe
from my desperation at midnight.
It's the most dangerous time. When
I'm about to give my body another
kind of relief is when I want to
eat. I give myself insomnia to stay
hungry. To stay thin. "Everything eaten
at night goes straight to your hips,
straight to your thighs," she said.
Hunger is but a way to treat myself
like my mother did, like one little
undeserving wretch. Hunger is my
husband, best friend, child. When I feel
alone or lonely, hunger will keep me
company. Rob me of my breasts, sure,
but also my sorrow in the night.
Hunger is caped, is the spawn of
thieves. Hollows my eyes, cheekbones,
clavicle, wrists, knees. Do you know
how many compliments I've gotten
on my collarbone since I started dying?
Hunger hangs her dress in the closet,
tempting me to go an inch, just an
inch, a meal, a pound, a day, a month,
a life closer to ultimate victory.

# LIZZIE BORDEN

*Lizzie Borden took an axe,*
*and gave her mother forty whacks.*
*When she saw what she had done*
*she gave her father forty one.*

—Popular rope-skipping rhyme

The axe handle gleamed from the corner, calling
Lizzie, Lizzie Borden, I am the shaft
made for your hands. Say yes and never

again will you have to wear his saliva
to school, or be tagged for sale by the slit
who made you. Imagine the perfect part

of the red sea upon their skulls. Feel forty
red whale eyes opening in the eight-limbed
creature called your parents. Open a horizon

in your blood line. Open an opening, an
aperture, an overture to your promise
to survive. Later, you can lick my glint

or eat the evidence like a barn cat eats
her afterbirth. Put yourself in the way
of your life, Lizzie. Wrench

yourself free of the blue cord noosing
you in the loft of their piety. Listen
to the swallows in the rafters. Don't they

canary in a coal mine? Don't they vulture
your carcass? What's it gonna be
yours or theirs? Don't be an un-

actress like your mother, Lizzie.
Be an artist. Pick up the handle
oiled with his lust. How many

times has he held me to your throat
while she might as well have
watched? Lizzie, don't be

a daughter, be an arm
upon which freedom swings; hell
be a soldier, be an axe, be a man.

# Homosexual Love

Dear God-fearing people, I am here to confess
that I have made homosexual love
to a chair! In the way God intended

me to use a chair, I have not. Instead,
I got on my knees and dove the muff
of a chair! If I were a homosexual,

and I am, I would make the best homosexual
love to chairs. Everywhere I went. In
the ladies' lounge at Macy's, for example.

While I waited for my tomato soup to cool
I would abominate the chaise lounge
in the name of my selfish non-procreative

pleasure. Me and the chaise lounge would
get it on! And then we would brush each
other's hair, look into the mirror

of each other's hauntingly similar reflections,
plot to steal Lot's wife. Introduce
her to a bar stool. Or worse—outdoor

furniture! So when Lot came home
from the rockery, he'd find his wife smoking
a cigarette with the umbrella table

on his back deck. I tell you, if I were a homosexual,
and I am, then you better watch out if you wanna
steal my chair. I mean, God-fearing good

people, I warn you now that when I come
to town you better lock up your wives, lock
up your children, you better lock up your chairs!

# Advice to a Trauma Survivor

Let your hinges wiggle
out of their holes. Strip

wood with your twisting. Honor
maggots, but not flies. Twist

tie everything you own
to everything you own. Elbow

to bicep. Torso to sternum. Faith
to the back of your hand. Slap

someone with the back of
your hand. Hold court with

no one watching but every
single one of your selves,

especially the runt. And her
little sister. Carry packages

over the river above your head,
even if reassured

they're water proof.
There are always leeches.

Carry salt. Salt their wicked
blind bodies. Use a match.

Careful not to burn your
fingers. But if you burn, relish.

Pain will make you pure
again. Talk into canisters

attached to strings, leading
to empty cans

of pumpkin in the ears of
your demons. Tell them

to slow down. Everyone needs
a vacation. To refresh

for life's purpose.
Tell a story to your littlest

demon. Rock her on your
knee. Whisper mosquito

sonnets into her coiled leaf
bones. When she falls into a deep

slumber, return her to her pride.
Even demons need their beauty

sleep. Feed yourself
like a mother bird

feeds her young.
Because the second time

around you might be able
to digest what you tell yourself.

Screw wheels
to the bottoms

of everything. Even
your knees. Even your hinges: don't tell them
                            they aren't bolts,
                            no one likes to
                            hear about *that*

sort of thing. Cover
your calluses. Toil.

No one should see you
work this hard to remain

vertical. Without chemical.
Repeat yourself

in list form. Drop
yourself in the grocery.

Someone will find you
and maybe rescue herself.

# TIME

Time's dress is made of corn husks, ripening, she is
always ripening. Dying she is always dying
and ripening. Time is unpeeled, unhusked by
tides. The moon simply one of her teeth
smoothed by years in the torrid waves.
Time's mood is almost always ironic. If you think it isn't,
wait     a while. Her music: whalesong spun backwards
through the phonograph funnels of her ears. Somewhere in the sea,
Time dropped her watch which is why she can't stop dancing. Can't stop
trying to outrun her father, who withholds his will
to part the sea to let her search along the bottom,
search for what belongs upon her wrist. So instead,
she misses curfew, stays out late with sailors,
storms. But certain to outlast them, Time is
careful not to fall in love.
She even sometimes in the moonlight sticks her neck
onto death's cutting board. But immune to sickle
Time simply sheds her head one husk at a time,
saunters towards an ever retreating
horizon she calls home.

# Rules of Having a Mistress

1. Keep her in a container under the bed to levitate your sad habit with your wife. Poke holes in the top of that lingerie box like you poke holes in your resolve to make honest women out of either of them.

2. Consider a third woman to balance things out. Chuckle at your own virility. How big must the greenhouse be of the man who has a mistress for his mistress? Consider this, but discard the idea because it interrupts the fallacy that love is the reason you can't choose between the forks in your tongue.

3. A degree in perfumery will come in handy for all the whiffs, the implications you'll be leaving in your wake. As will a degree in literature or philosophy in order to say so much without saying anything at all, even when pinned down.

4. Keep a kernel of corn in your back pocket. The starving mouth to which you feed it will have already convinced herself it's a full meal, will act accordingly grateful. Never, ever, deal in full cobs. Full cobs are for those not cut out for deprivation as a means to a greater greenhouse.

5. Fashion a story around the word victim. Spin it to yourself, your mistress, your therapist, your distant friend in whom you confide. Distant because she knows none of the players and isn't liable to slip. Plus, she's next in line.

## Pussy Christ

If there were a Pussy Christ,
he would be you. The resurrected

dead article son of the divine. I,
willing to wash the whole plum skin

of you with my hair, suckle
your toes like watermelon prayers

on Sundays under blankets, upstairs
below ceiling fan, in attic, salvage

ourselves past bedtime just to whisper
each other dreams. My shoulders rotate

just enough to catch a glimpse
of me through the strawberry patch

of your eyes. You are ungodly
August. Our hands match. Holding

them makes me want to swim under the dawn,
reach for piety, have you slap

me for it. I am your mistress, your devoted
nun, your whore, your wife.

# GREEN ONIONS

In the way of my desire are two thick farmer's hands,
thumbnails split from too much time in the earth, my

earth, my acidic earth. His hands full of me and mouth
full of onions. What gets in the way are my scars. Literal,

not figurative. What does it mean to have scars on my
vagina? On the inside, the canal, the fleshy wet, not-so-

wet because his hands, his teeth are in the way of my
desire? What does it mean to have these scars?

I've never met anyone with scars on the inside
of her vagina. Let alone ones put there by her father's

capable farmer's split thumb growing onions, little
green onions that he stuffs in his mouth with soft

bread and margarine, onion sandwich. "Want one?"
he asks. I shake my head, cover my scars.

What gets in the way of my desire is my proclivity
for little green onions. I like the way their stalks give

way in the wind, and how their taut little heads burst
into song in my mouth. The way they cry and scream

all the way to my stomach trying to punch
their way out punch their way out.

What gets in the way of my desire are little
green onions stuffed in my vagina hissing

their acidic hiss. My thick unsplit farmer's
daughter's hands useless to pull them out.

# GIN

Isn't that what we're all carrying? A second
skin like the topography of a soiled paper sack
around a bottle of gin? It's been a long time
since I breathed rancid pine needle breath
into the night air of my saturated bedroom,
but I still carry around me that sheath. That
attempt to hide without being able to hide
what's underneath, a vehicle of escape
that's slowly killing me. Ounce by ounce.
Proof by proof. The closer to pure
can gamble you blind, but I never
feared grain alcohol like I was supposed
to, like I shouldn't imbibe what someone's
corn pipe uncle brewed in the shed. In fact,
I craved it. Craved what men with split
hands, split shoes, split tongues could mix
and mash and distill into a story
about a people who wanted, on some days,
to shrink right out of their washed-too-many-
times-to-ever-look-clean-overalls.
Who wanted to shuck the paper sack
that gave them away as shameful, liquid
sin. Those of us born to be liquid sin
are born into lolling-eyed wrath
into tobacco streams between our teeth
down our chins, dripping off necks
down the glossy outside of our shatterable
bottles, our shatterable bodies. No matter
how many years I've been sober, I won't
ever be able to wring that stench, that
breath out of me. Catch me without gum
in my mouth, and it means I trust you
enough to let you smell what I am
made of: sin, gin, and desire
to inebriate anything animate or able
to feel right through my pores out
of my skin. I am a bottle, break me
and all I'll do is soak in, soak in.

# WIDOW

I could smell her on you, your trick.
The too sweet perfume she left on your
back. When you put your stack

of bills on the night table and turned
your animal eyes towards me
in the half light, I felt a scythe

in my side. For what you'd lost.
Only you know what it is. But I had
a sense that the menses of your youth

had passed through the thighs of night.
I'd like to say that while you were
gone, I dug nails into my palms.

But the truth is I slept, knowing I could
keep nothing from slipping through
my impotent knuckles. In the morning,

given the circumstance, I didn't offer
my breast, but instead undid my
hair, pushed oil into your gooseflesh.

By then you'd showered. Which made
me sad. That you thought you had to.
But happy that you might smell yourself

on yourself. That is if I were able
to raise your salt to the surface. Before
you showered, you curled

your fingers away from my kiss, but
I didn't smell her on them. Only you.
And the cash steaming on the nightside

table. You might have sniffed your
fist, had it been inside me all night
more than metaphorically. But

I'm not built like that. And nine
hours would need to pass before
you formed a fist. In traffic.

I wanted to ask what your trigger smelled
like. But I didn't. I think we both know
the bouquet crushed inside it. She.

Who is not exactly the other woman.
I don't want to say I want to
kill her, but I want to say I don't

want to not kill her either.
Her desperation makes me
sick. Her menopause makes

me sick. Her wealth makes me want
to burn a city. Including its
youth. I'd like to make the city eat

its youth, but that's how this
whole thing got started,
isn't it? With a widow

spidering her way into our sheets.
If only as an aftertaste. They say
cyanide smells like almonds.

# Outside My Face

### I. To My Husband's Mistress

When you slither-backed into our bed I didn't recognize you at
first, was just so grateful for the return of hunger to our night.
My slip around my shoulders, unaware I was but a sarcophagus
with a pulse, drain in the right place. I should have looked closer
to see your tongue darting out from the pipe in the lowest part of
the ground.

### II. To the Wife of the Man I'm Fucking

Before you were even on your back, he was thinking of me.
Parting the continent of your thighs, he was licking me from his
lips. Lucky our names are the same, but for one consonant.

### III. To the Man I'm Fucking

I always knew you were mine, but the discovery of being your
mistress is like a hole in my cheek I didn't know was there. I kept
wondering why all my food ended up outside my face.

# YOUR MISSING

Is shaped like a mouth,
a mewl. Is a mewling.
Measures the size of a fist.
Weighs a finite number
of ounces. But whoever
put it there is not walking
around with the rest
of you in his pockets,
though many of us will spend
our lives searching behind
zippers with our mouths
for what we're

missing. A mewl is different
than a meow: it's more sad,
"Mewl." Painting it to look
like a flower will work
for a while, attract
onlookers, but also
bees. To cover with curtains
could work but leave
you lonely which, of course,
is already outlining the body
bag of your Missing's flat

pulse. Plenty of people
will want to retreat
into their Missing. Erect
monuments to its beauty.
Let them. Sometimes
it's good to be lied to. Feeds.
Sometimes being lied
to is food. "Like, there's nothing
wrong with you, you're perfect.
It's not you, it's me."

Your Missing is hairless.
Susceptible to the wind. Howls.
The best advice is to tend
to it alone. Drawing attention
to your Missing will have people
put you back on the shelf.
Where you will go on sale.
Be vulnerable to strangers
who are willing to settle

for a bargain. You will be shaped
like a bargain. Half price. Orange
tag painted flower begging
under blue light mewling
with a heartbeat pick me,
pick me, pick me.

# Hey, World

"Hey, World, you look great in those boots. Is that a new purse?"

"World, I've been meaning to tell you, you look great in fuchsia, and not many people can pull off pink."

"Smile, World! Hey, give us a little smile. Worlds are prettier when they smile."

"Can I have your phone number, World?"

"World, where you walkin' so fast?"

"Did I ever tell you how much I like yellow? That dress makes me wanna leave my wife."

"World, whyn't you take off those shades so I can see those pretty eyes."

"Nice legs, World. Those are what you call a tall glass of come sit by me."

"Do you have a light?"

"Can I give you a ride?"

"Are those real? I mean real-real?"

"World, do you have a boyfriend? Lu-kee GUY! But is he built like me? I mean can he satisfy? A World like you needs some satisfaction."

"World, you shouldn't talk like that it's not becoming. Oh, you don't mean that."

"Ha ha! Listen to the mouth on that little World. Man-o-man what a feisty World. I like my Worlds feisty. Better in bed when they fightcha just a little."

"See you tomorrow, World. I'll be right here waitin' for you to walk by."

# Sex from the Perspective of My Hair

When she loosens
us from the twist
on her head
we know it's coming.
We know the sweat
of his thigh will paste
us to the side of her face
from where he will
eventually un-paste us
with a finger
and his thank you.

But before that we
know for a musical
moment we will rock
as one weed under
water with the rhythm
of his hips to the pulse
of her suckle
when we do that for long
enough, some of us,
an unpredictable
few of us, a school
of strands will give up
our roots, remain
in his hand, pressed
into palm long after
she has re-twisted
us into our tower,
our perch, where we
will wait again
for him to wink.

# HER OWN ROAD

Before I broke the spine of my daughterhood
over the hood of my accelerating car, I

considered your corpse. What it would feel
like to see you in the casket, cheeks roughed

to a color they never were, eyes sewn shut
with fishing wire. Flesh hard as if bone

had grown all the way to the surface. Before
I christened my new life by breaking the carafe

of your motherhood over the hull of my freedom, I
considered your corpse. All the reasons you never

gave now frozen in the brick that used to be
your brain. I considered that I'd never hear how

much you missed me. But would always know how much
you missed me. Without being able,

in an entire Universe, to estimate the size of the hole
I left in the galaxy of family. I destroyed

the orbits, interrupted centrifugal force. Before I left, I
considered gravity, and its cousin inertia,

decided you weren't worth either, and I was better
than both. Now, at the center of my own solar system

of smithereens, I find myself wondering who, before
she leaves home, will ever consider my casket, break

the carafe of my madness over the hull of her freedom
in search of her own road.

# FUCK CHRISTMAS

Fuck Christmas! I mean, all that happy family
yule log fat man down the chimney bullshit,
fuck it! Fuck the tree, fuck the lights, fuck
the manger, the Messiah, the frankincense
and the myrrh. Fuck the little wrapping paper
paper cuts. Fuck the holly. Fuck the fa,
fuck the la, not to mention the la la la la la.

Fuck the motherfucking cranberry. Fuck the
mistletoe! Double fuck the mistletoe. Shuck
the leaves off and fuck the dead stem. Seriously,
do you have any idea how annoying Christmas is
to anyone who doesn't have a family? Nineteen
years since anyone's offered me any Folger's
fuckin' crystals. So, fuck that song, that little
bastard of an "I'll be home for…" Fuck the
dude who wrote it. And while you're at it,
fuck Burl Ives and those little claymation elves.
Fuck the abominable snowman. No, he's pretty
cool, you can unfuck him. But fuck Rudolph!
That's what I said, butt-fuck Rudolph
in his saving Santa sleigh.

And then fuck the fat man's wife. 'Cause
don't you imagine she needs it? All that merry
merry up on a rooftop all year on repeat's gotta
drive her insane. Now, there's a woman who,
long about December 24th has gotta be thinking,
"Jesus, what's it take to get a little Marvin Gaye
up in this bitch?" Seriously, if only for the Missus,
don't you think it's high time we all fuck Christmas?

# Rain Saws At

the window.
Coffee tastes
like a puddle.
Ones from which
I'd stand
back when the
school bus came.
The neighbor's dog licks

himself, his tumor
swells with each swipe.
I can't help but wonder
when the seals
on the skylight
will give. In will
march the Morton
Salt girl, scalpel in her
hand. When it rains,
it's Washington.
When it pours,

it's malignant.
The whole time
she had it, I couldn't
say it. Tumor
somehow more polite
than cancer. She had
cancer. Now that she's
gone, died is more
polite than dead.
What kind of rain

would you call
this? Pelting?
Slicing? When
she stopped eating,
the vet said I could

feed her a slurry
of water and grain.
The smell is still all
over my floor, bed,
hands. It wakes
me up at night, has
me claw at the insides
of my nostrils. The only
time it doesn't

reek inside me
is when my mouth
pours with tears. Which
isn't very often.
Despair salt-bagged
by fear. Of never
stopping. Yesterday,
the sky held
its threat. Dirty
and dark with rain, but

stubborn as an
old dog learning
to play dead.

# Too Early

The ones who've been fucked too early
are beautiful. The way their hinges hang

from their hips, frames without doors. Doors
lost long ago, knobs and all. Breezes

breathe through them in places      that whistle
conversely, tissue twisted so tightly

ribbons of scars trail behind. The way we lean
like we're gonna fall

over, but don't. The way our love
is like an earthquake—

nothing that lives beyond
is ever the same. I love that we're open-

eyed, not afraid of anything because we've already
been sucked up by the storm and spit

out. To live beyond being beached
by a tornado is bound to produce a freak

child with too much light
in her eyes, not enough cotton in her

ears. We hear everything. Can accommodate
all of you, but only if we want to. There's not another

like the one who's been done too early. Not another
YES as open as the heartland sky, or a mouth mid-

scream. Our hearts are mouths mid-scream, swim
inside our ribs at your own, and only, risk.

# ADVICE TO ANYONE
# LOVING A TRAUMA SURVIVOR

What I love about being an incest survivor
are the tourists! The ones who want to know what it's like
to fuck a girl who's actually fucked her father. "I know,
maybe I can get her to call me 'daddy' while doin'
the deed!" They bring their headlamps, laminated
maps, wide lens cameras slapping their diaphragms.
They press palms up to the glass, despite the zookeeper's,
"Warning! Don't feed the G-Spot or she's likely to

rip your arm off!" Dear anyone loving a trauma survivor,
my best advice is this: stay still. Until she beckons.
Do not approach her like she's made of glass. Do
fashion a rubber floor, if only for your own ego.
If you're lucky, when the lights are off, she will beg
you to at once, forget she is an incest survivor, but
never forget she is an incest survivor. Do this
and shatter her defense. Never wield the pieces

at anything but your own flaming heart. Aim for blue.
She will know you're lying if you only go for yellow.
Bring your fingertips. Run them through the flame. Don't
flinch. It's the only thing she'll trust. Your triumph:
that word ever breaking bread with her mouth.

# CROW FUNERAL

We witnessed a funeral, a murder
of crows in the trees. Cawing
the story to their congregation of how

fledgling's neck went limp at the pot-
of-gold end to his first flight.
I was saddened by their loss,

but couldn't hide glee that your boots
made that sound against cement
meaning you were next

to me. Once, you told me you liked
my shirt, but that it would look better
on the floor. I winced, but it wasn't

that moment I threw myself out
of the nest, it was another. The day
I caught the forward arc

of your arm and there, holding
your forearm above your belt,
I couldn't help but wonder what

sound the buckle would make
against the floor. When my people sing
of me, I hope they tell the story

of how I was beautiful once,
so stunning in flight that every borne
moment was worth my neck.

# A Femme Is
*After Roma Raye*

A femme is a bitch.
A bitch is a dog. Dog.
A femme is a spike.
A spike is a tool.
          Tool.

A tool is a weapon.
Necessary. A weapon
is necessary. A dog
is a tool. To hound or
          herd.

A femme herds or breeds.
Femme breeds danger.
Brings male gaze.
Gaze is a threat.
          Femme

is a threat. Threat is a fist.
Through glass. Pieces into
spikes. Spike bitch spike.
A tool is a stone.
          Butch

through a window. Thrown.
Butch on a throne. Femme
is a window. Bark, tool,
bark. A bark is not a toy.
          Toy

is a mouth. A femme
is a mouth. A butch is
a bite. Breed gaze femme.
Butch bone
          bite.

Bone is a treat.
Drool toy drool.
Bark bitch drool.
Dog femme
            spike.

# The Day I Accidentally Caused the Death of a Baby Sunfish and My Mother Called Me a Murderer

And the sky held
off the clouds
while the air
dried to a crisp
fin. My bathing
suit turned gummy
against my skin
while the lake stood
still, only halfway
to my knees. Still
so sediments stirred
by my feet weren't washed
away but lingered
like a cloud
of dark blood.

# MENTAL ILLNESS

All the walls
are turning to dust. All
the hands have eyes.
The towel rack
isn't enough to keep
me standing. The telephone
is a knife. Promises
are hot coils of burners
against my face
in my mother's eyes
that still roil in my stomach
any time I'm asked
to trust.

I've swallowed
my mother's eyes.
They're part of every one
of my gut instincts.
She was always near-
sighted. Me, farsighted
but I've developed
a fear of my glasses.

Mental illness,
something we whisper
at tables, hide under
napkins like we haven't
all been wolves at one
break or another. The snap,
crack of a limb
split and I'm hiding
from the window

again. It's not so
much that I don't
like the view as
I don't want anyone
to see in. Where did I put
my feet? Is that the dog
stirring or tomorrow
poking my throat?

# String

My body is a house to string, strung enough to wrap around

a harbor song in the center somewhere a tambourine somewhere

a cymbal clap an orange slice shivering in sections behind my

ear. Lick my neck and taste salt. But lick my ear and taste every holy

citrus of every Florida grove. I used to be a bee until I left

my stinger in a girl behind the Gulf station. She shouted into my bandana

I captured it with my palm, pocketed her exultation drove my green

Chevy truck sixty miles past home to ask my grandma for some string.

# WELCOME HERE
*for Chase*

Your jagged is welcome
here. Your protrusion.
Your concavity. To both
I cup my ear, take in awe-
breath. Your smooth, your
sand, your slick, your sticky,
your cells that rigid them-
selves under my touch, swell
their chests, begin to boast
about what they have
in store for us. For me,

their bestowing of honor, for you
their neural bounty. Let yourself
be. Bring every shape you take,
they are welcome at this feast.

For the places we do or do not
have angles, do or do not have
curves, do or do not exhibit
our mammalian biology,
we should not be blamed.

What I mean to say
is that breasts are no more
inherently gendered than fingernails.
They can be all genders or none,
but never nothing, because your
very mass is sacred, sexy,

safe. If I could I would take all of you
into my rocking, seething center
where I can't help but
be glad that you don't flatten out.

# CRAYFISH

I never begged my parents to stop
beating my brother. Tear stained,
he would plead with them to stop
hitting me. I would stand there wolf–
eyed, my shoulder my father's
shoulder, his forearm my forearm,
my palm stinging and happy
with every blow. My mother only ever
slapped his ass, and never hard enough
to make my palm sting, but I wanted her to
beat the living tar out of him. I wanted her
to beat him as hard as she was proving she
loved me. I was her favorite, but
she loved him more. Her eyes teacups
overflowing with his innocence, his good,
good little boy heart. Me, I was a girl, stunk
between the legs. Any time she was ever
in a single stall restroom with me,
she'd say, "Your piss stinks."
I'd hold it until there was blood
in my urine to steer clear of my mother
having to smell my void.

There was a crayfish I kept in a jar
on top of the out of tune piano for
months. I had snatched her from the
lake in the spring when stuck to her
underside were several hundred eggs.
As we watched them hatch, my third
grade class asked me as many questions
as there were births. I was as important
as a doctor. A week later, I doled them out
like gumdrops to be taken home to their
not-in-my-house parents. None of them
lived by a lake and I knew it. Still,
I sent them home with baggies full
of tap water and infant crustaceans.

Then I scooped the mother into a
peanut butter jar, carried her home
on the bus. My mother kept telling me
to take her outside before she died, to let her
loose in the lake, but I didn't want to pour
out my classmates admiration of me. Not
looking up from my book, I'd say, "I will."

The jar was too small for her claws;
she stood on her haunches for weeks,
her single antennae bowing in rhythm
like steady blinks of her beady lidless
eyes. Once in a while I'd check on her
before I went to bed, but only long enough
to make sure the antennae still indicated
underwater life. When the antennae drooped
like a passed out dancing girl against
the glass, I panickedly snatched up the jar,
undid the rusty lid to smell my own piss.

The empty corpse of her oddly blue shell
slid easily into the lake. As I watched her
drift, belly up, all the way to the bottom,
I rinsed the jar, spit in it and rinsed again.
Neither one of her claws unstuck themselves
from their rigor mortis haunch. I told
myself that if I, her tormentor, stopped
watching, maybe she'd come back
to life. But I couldn't take my eyes off
her as the current mimicked the motion
of her helpless legs. Each pulse
a careful well arched swoop of my father's
arm against my brother's bare, barely able
to take him without breaking like glass
upper thighs. My eyes grew beady
in their sockets, locked on the wish for him
to break. I swallowed what it tasted like
to have someone beg for me with all his
little boy heart. Freshwater gone piss,
rotten as dead fish in my mouth.

# REGRET

is a call that comes in the middle
            of the night. She says, are you sleeping?
You're not sleeping. You're
            counting. You're an accountant

of infractions, steps you took this
            way instead of that. This is how she teaches
you to dance on your own tomb. While bite sizes
            of who you could have been fly

over on stringed wings. Is there a sadder instrument
            than the open mouth of a violin
you could have played but didn't? Yes, it's called
            the harmonica of holes you drilled

in your life. Or into the lives of those you've
            loved. Can you remember the teeth
of everyone you've made cry? The imprint
            of their embouchures on your character? Think

of them before they were stripped
            of their bouquets, before you showed
your true face. The one on loan from your own
            betrayer. Remember his teeth? How perfectly

they fit in your heart? Were you
            small then? Were you blue? Were you a set
of musical strings? Was he the bow? What tune
            did you learn to hum in his arms?

Was he holding a harmonica in his pocket? A beast
            under his chin? Does his phone ring in the middle
of the night. When he answers, is it your voice
            asking if he's sleeping?

# MISTRESS

It's not surprising, given that I was my father's
mistress, that I'd choose to be
mistressed again and again. Not chosen

but for the nugget of lust, the ancillary erection
I provide for someone not really intending to veer
from the vector of his real life. Now, I could cough

up a hairball of fury for those who've been willing
to mistress me, and they would deserve it, but
that's not really the point. The point

is that wrapped around my phantom
cock like a second foreskin is my willingness
to mistress myself. To step right into that harlot's second

hand lingerie. Have you ever worn a bra you bought
at a thrift store but no matter how many washings
you couldn't remove the original owner's

smell? But the thing was so damn hot
I mean, made you drip
into your shoes you couldn't not

wear it. You try to cover up her stench with your own
perfume, but at the end of your night
you peel the thing off to find your own sweat

smells like her, smells
like the wife. I am that bra. I smell like the wife, but
I'm not the original, just a whiff of one.

# Along the Fault Line

Somewhere along the fault
>line lays the preposterous idea that I forgive myself.

# YOUR THROAT

in my grip is opera before
it finds the stage.
Your throat is the spotlight.
Your throat is the
cast, the conductor, the
orchestra, the pulse of
the leading man taken
with two fingers as the
crescendo threatens to
bring down the chandeliers.
Your throat is my cock
out of which I will choke
an orgasm. Shoot the
moon with how much
I want to Break. You.
In. Your throat is the animal
before it becomes
hide, the soft plea to be
stitched into boot enough
to kick the door down
to where you've been
hiding. Hoping–praying
I find you. Hoping-
praying I don't come
for you. Against your
"no" huddled inside the
"o" is a small tremendous
wish that I will, won't
open my belt, slip it around
your neck, tighten
until you see God.

# Parrot in a Pear Tree

Maybe it's not that I didn't want
a child. Maybe it's that I didn't want a child

with you. Certainly, your rattling hands
on my tallest shoulders sent the dream fluttering

into the night, like a frightened parrot screeching
from the tree, refusing to come down. After which

I started shrinking. Cutting nuts in half, throwing
away the larger half. The lady I pay to love me

says, "Maybe you started starving because he was
trying to devour you." A broken bell thunks in a tower.

A dog with one front paw pokes at the door. Now
that you're on your way with another "crazy

woman," chuckle chuckle over your propensity to lick
what's unstable, to joyride nitroglycerin, I find these walls

suddenly growing mouths. Even my house is hungry. So, feed
that new braying wolf your genes. Feed her your loose

change to make her rattle. Feed her a future made of luncheons
thick with middle-class mothers, but leave me to eat

the dirt. Wolf I will. Along with every world of seed that waits
in it. Let me sprout into a pear tree. Parrot from my own branch,

"I am free, I am free, I am free!"

# Uncommon Woman

*And after nine years of marriage my husband says he wants to be married to
a woman he loves less, because he thinks he'll be less lonely when she's away.
Plus, she's not always out at poetry readings.*

For any woman who's ever been told she's too much:

You, who broke out of the mold before they even cracked it
off you. You, who came out inventing your own how-to-scale-a-wall
with only vowels. You, who fireflash in the eye of so many

midnights, so many men who want to taste your hem, who dream
of being desired by an Uncommon Woman, if only because
their dressers are empty of anything but name brand cologne

and predictable portrait. Let them call you different. Let them bait
the minnows of your heart. Show them your heart is a school
of fish, a solar system of all moons. When asked, say,

"My heart is always causing the mating season." When they call you
full of yourself, say, "Yes." Breathe in their scorn and breathe out
Atlantis. Let them come with their saw blade smiles. Let them come

with their saw blade hands. Let them come to see if you slice
small enough to replace their handkerchiefs, the ones they'll loan
to who they'll call easier girls. Let them choose easier girls.

When he tells you he is tossing your broken root out his open window,
and holds up to the glass a more common woman, surrender. Gracefully
surrender the pretend olive branch of his matrimony. The pretend

complete protein he slipped onto your third finger while you stood
in shoes that were always too small for you. When he says she is easier
to handle, live with, attach to, fuck, I want you to remember your neck.

The way it ascends space, and always has, above the rest. You were brought
here for so much more than walking two by two up a ship plank. Anyone
common enough to go coward at the depth of his love for you, wasn't meant

to walk beside you. So go live in the liquid bowl of gold you were handed for a skin. Uncommon Woman, let the easier girls pick up the socks. Embrace your splendid singularity. And look to the rest of us Uncommon Women

standing in the centers, holding up the tents of our skirts, we call them cities. Love should not have us stoop to fit a portrait. Love should have us elevate our infinity. So, Uncommon Woman, don't settle for less.

Instead, stride towards the ever shedding horizon. Take her example of renewal. Wear your grief like a party dress! Remember, the sun's only lover is not the Earth. She's got moons on every planet.

# EVENTUALLYS

When all of your eventuallys have come
to roost, carried their pigeon wings over
your mother's shame garden, some
of them will sound like hallelujah, others
like hope to heaven never, all
of them will leave their footprints
in the kitchen of your unforgivens.

# DANDELIONS

There is a strangling patch of dandelions
in my driveway which isn't even really
a driveway but a patch of asphalt butting

up against the alley where scared girls
and bold dealers make the rounds
at night. Girls skitter like birds, would hop

over garbage cans if they saw you
see them. The dandelions are closed
at night when the girls walk by. Have

folded up their bounty into dragon snouts
of green leather, holding their fire inside.
By day, dandelions do what dandelions

can't be stopped from doing. In fact, murder
one and they send in their extended families
to put their tap roots into fragile ground

all around your yard, until they even grow
out from under the fence into the alley.
As if to say paradise was crowded.

The girls, they pick the dandelions.
Milky blood stains their hands dark.
They press hollow stalks into tight

fists, where they wilt before they get them
into a jar of water to unceremoniously expire.
The dealers, they pluck them too, tickle girls'

chins with blooms, promising if the petals
turn her skin yellow it means she likes butter.
We believe in butter, have some

butter. Come on over here
paradise is melting for you chickadee.
I've put it on the stove for you, just for you.

# Mother's Day

*On Mother's Day, 2009, she tells me she's moving back in with him. Her head will hit the yellowed pillow beside his every night. I've never seen her buy a new pillow. Last year I brought her a giant wildly blooming pink plant. I think it was a primrose. Nineteen years had passed, and I wanted something to thrust into her arms when she started clutching at me on her doorstep. It worked.*

Dear Mother,

I never wear pink. It's the color of little girls, and I'm afraid of the dark. I sleep in a tree house. When no one is next to me I jam a chair under the door knob and pray to the Gods who decide who's been raped enough to pass over me this time. Cross my fingers they'll ignore someone else's blood covenant. But I wouldn't wish this on anyone.

Tell me, does the primrose bloom? Does it go with the curtains? The ones you stitched in the boiler room turned into quilting den. Do you prick your finger, bring the salt to your mouth, or do you wear protection on your thumb? I know you don't believe me. But how else would I know that he uses Gold Trojans?

You must not remember the doctor who had to yank my vagina apart where it was growing together from the friction when I was eight. From the friction when I was ten. From the friction when I was twelve. When I was thirteen I thanked God that I was too old to keep going to that doctor. You must not remember how he instructed you to use Vaseline and your fingers to keep the hole open for weeks after the yanking.

Dear Mother, I think I might be straight, but the scars won't let a man inside me. It's not that I haven't found one who doesn't mind, but I can't face my own grief that I can't give him his biological destiny. Can't offer him safe harbor no matter how drunk I try. I'm sober now, so the trying's stopped. Thank God a girl finally pushed her tongue into my mouth, so I could feel something other than incapable.

Dear Mother, primroses grow best in moist, slightly acidic soil. My partner wants a baby, but I don't think it's responsible for me to call myself anything more than far too acidic, and anyway, the wanting of one I buried years ago. I know you remember his roses. How he fertilized them at the root with fish heads buried deep. Their dead eyes pushing perfume into our summers.

Dear Mother, you were a child when he plucked you. Half his age when the other half of my chromosomes leaked into your knee socks. I forgave you long ago. But when you sleep next to him, breathe his night air, I want you to remember how we loved each other once. Me, your knight in shining primroses whose steed you've let for forty years pass by.

Dear Mother, I know you're moving in to help him die. And I don't wish a hard or any death on him. In fact, I've forgiven him. It's just that I can't forgive myself long enough to let a body near me without thrusting something wild in between us. That, and I would still give an eye to watch you lay your head on a brand new pillow.

# Peace and Justice

When peace comes it will not be on the wing of a dove,
but on a wave of one hundred thousand million foaming
tongues. She will ride the dirty water
of held back vengeance, surf over centuries
of violence that we have all called justice.
But justice will have to leave his boots
at her doorstep, take the latch key from around
his neck, enter her house on his knees.

What are you willing to give up for peace?

Have you made any with your wolves? Have you
forgiven your father? If you want the Palestinians
and Israelis to stop, then have you sent a Christmas ham
to the man who beat your mother? Distasteful,
repugnant, he will nonetheless be among those
huddled in the house of humanity when peace comes.
To make her house our house we may have to dig
forks into our palms under tables heaped with ill-gotten bounty.

I don't know if I'm willing.

Which is to say, I don't know if I've readied
myself for her residence in my heart. The list of those
against whom I hold grudges grows as I breathe.
As I breathe, I am an American, and therefore believe
in heroes, sink my claws into competition. I want to be the first
one over the finish line photographed while tongue-kissing
my enemy if only to see my picture on the front page
of forever. I want to be that martyr, because for an American

what is furthest from monster? When I hold up my hands
I want the pope to be able to eat from them while he
congratulates me. What are my motives?
In my best moments I want my father, my rapist,
to eat bountifully from his own hands.
Don't I think I'm noble for this? But could I

welcome the idea of his orgasm? What would it take
for me to want my father to, without shame,
receive his God-given right to bodily pleasure?
Who would I have to be to be that invested in peace?

What am I made of?

Girl. Times rape. Times the fists of lovers in my face.
Times poverty equals the white dress of Victimry.
I've sold my vows to the ferryboat man so he could
rush me to the bank emblazoned with Not Guilty. But
what kind of horrible pain have I caused my father by telling
the world my version of him? If you don't think this keeps
me up at night, then maybe you think I don't have a heart. Maybe
the queen stole it, replaced it with that of a swine. I used to think

the most horrible part is that I still love him, that I couldn't
suck him out of my DNA. But maybe, it's the most magnificence
ever bestowed upon me by the mistress of peace. Maybe in her tattered
gown she will escort me over her doorstep on the day I send my father
flowers. Thank him for the beautiful scar out of which to carve myself.

What am I willing to sacrifice?

I will tell you, my life. But what if what's required for us all to breach
the doorstep of peace is to shuck the carapace of our grudges,
liquid all of humanity into a new, complicated, carved
out of our scars, relationship to forgiveness?

# LIFE STORY

My life story in 24 words:
Green shoot, raze rape,
strawberry wound,
vodka, vodka, vodka,
pussy. Steeple, oh
steeple, corner me
with my mouth tilted up
to syllables gone chimes.

My life story in 12 words
taken from the original 24:
Oh, vodka, rape
strawberry with tilted
syllables. Shoot steeple,
shoot mouth. Up.

My life story in 6 words:
Steeple. Mouth.
Rape strawberry vodka.
Tilted.

3 words:
rape
strawberry
mouth

My life story in 1 word:
Faced with choosing
between rape and mouth,
I choose strawberry.

# ABOUT THE AUTHOR

**Tara Hardy** is the working class queer femme poet who founded Bent, a writing institute for LGBTIQ people in Seattle, Washington. She is a founding member of Salt Lines, the all woman performance poetry group that tours internationally. By a vote of the people, the Seattle City Council named Tara Hardy Seattle Poet Populist in 2002. She is the recipient of the 2011 Washington Poets Association Burning Word Award, and is a member of the Saints and Sinners Literary Festival Hall of Fame. Tara has been finalist on seven National Poetry Slam stages. A daughter of the United Auto Workers, and activist in the Battered Women's Movement, Tara is committed to art as a tool for social change. Her work has been published in various journals and anthologies, including the two anthologies by Seal Press, *Sex and Single Girls* and *Without A Net*. Tara is a keynote speaker and performer on hundreds of campuses for Take Back the Night, LGBT Pride, Women's History Month, Trans Awareness Week, Kink on Campus, Women's Studies and Lavender graduations, Domestic Violence Awareness Month, National Coming out Day, and various gender, sexuality, social class, and poetry related events. She teaches workshops on topics such as gender identity, healing from sexual assault through writing, post-assault sexuality, performance poetry, erotic writing, being a working class artist, eating disorders, domestic violence, and anti-oppression/liberation. Currently, Tara writes within view of majestic Mt. Rainier, but she misses the great big Michigan sky that reared her. To contact Tara, or arrange for a performance, email wordyfemme@hotmail.com. Her webpage is www.tarahardy.net.

# ACKNOWLEDGMENTS

Thank you Write Bloody for choosing me. Thank you Derrick Brown for all you do for poets.

Thank you Dorothy Allison, Sini Anderson, Daemond Arrindell, Patch Avery, Corrina Bain, Bent, Rocky Bernstein, Sevan Boult, Kate Bornstein, Sara Brickman, Greg Brisendine, Francois Camoin, Debbie Carlsen, Jason Carney, Amy Cornell, Ivan Coyote, Jacob D'Annunzio, Vicki D'Annunzio, Allison Durazzi, Elaina M. Ellis, Karen Finneyfrock, Paula Friedrich, Andrea Gibson, Maya Hersh, Martin Horn, Natalie Illum, Denise Jolly, Alvin Lau, Diane Lefer, Carol Lellis, Dee Matthews, Rachel McKibbens, Kathleen Nacozy, Poetry Slam, Inc., Lacey Phoenix Roop, Roy Seitz, Denise Sheppard, Tristan Silverman, Sonya Rene Taylor, Michelle Tea, Tryka D. Tryka, Fran Varian, Jeanann Verlee, Vermont College, Buddy Wakefield, Chase Williams, Eric Zachmann. This book, and my survival, would not be possible without you.

A very special thank you to Tamara Lewis who is every balm, spitfire and torchlight that ever the mending should need.

# NEW WRITE BLOODY BOOKS FOR 2011

*Dear Future Boyfriend*
Cristin O'Keefe Aptowicz's debut collection of poetry tackles
love and heartbreak with no-nonsense honesty and wit.

*38 Bar Blues*
C. R. Avery's second book, loaded with bar-stool musicality and brass-knuckle poetry.

*Workin' Mime to Five*
Dick Richard's is a fired cruise ship pantomimist. You too can learn
his secret, creative pantomime moves. Humor by Derrick Brown.

*Reasons to Leave the Slaughter*
Ben Clark's book of poetry revels in youthful discovery from the heartland
and the balance between beauty and brutality.

*Yesterday Won't Goodbye*
Boston gutter punk Brian Ellis releases his second book of poetry,
filled with unbridled energy and vitality.

*Write About an Empty Birdcage*
Debut collection of poetry from Elaina M. Ellis that flirts with loss,
reveres appetite, and unzips identity.

*These Are the Breaks*
Essays from one of hip-hops deftest public intellectuals, Idris Goodwin

*Bring Down the Chandeliers*
Tara Hardy, a working-class queer survivor of incest, turns sex,
trauma and forgiveness inside out in this collection of new poems.

*The Feather Room*
Anis Mojgani's second collection of poetry explores storytelling and
poetic form while traveling farther down the path of magic realism.

*Love in a Time of Robot Apocalypse*
Latino-American poet David Perez releases his first book
of incisive, arresting, and end-of-the-world-as-we-know-it poetry.

*The New Clean*
Jon Sands' poetry redefines what it means to laugh, cry, mop it up and start again.

*Sunset at the Temple of Olives*
Paul Suntup's unforgettable voice merges subversive surrealism
and vivid grief in this debut collection of poetry.

*Gentleman Practice*
Righteous Babe Records artist and 3-time International Poetry Champ
Buddy Wakefield spins a nonfiction tale of a relay race to the light.

*How to Seduce a White Boy in Ten Easy Steps*
Debut collection for feminist, biracial poet Laura Yes Yes
dazzles with its explorations into the politics and metaphysics of identity.

*Hot Teen Slut*
Cristin O'Keefe Aptowicz's second book recounts stories of
a virgin poet who spent a year writing for the porn business.

*Working Class Represent*
A young poet humorously balances an office job with the life
of a touring performance poet in Cristin O'Keefe Aptowicz's third book of poetry

*Oh, Terrible Youth*
Cristin O'Keefe Aptowicz's plump collection commiserates and celebrates
all the wonder, terror, banality and comedy that is the long journey to adulthood.

# OTHER WRITE BLOODY BOOKS (2003 - 2010)

*Great Balls of Flowers (2009)*
Steve Abee's poetry is accessible, insightful, hilarious, compelling,
upsetting, and inspiring. TNB Book of the Year.

*Everything Is Everything (2010)*
The latest collection from poet Cristin O'Keefe Aptowicz,
filled with crack squirrels, fat presidents, and el Chupacabra.

*Catacomb Confetti (2010)*
Inspired by nameless Parisian skulls in the catacombs of France,
Catacomb Confetti assures Joshua Boyd's poetic immortality.

*Born in the Year of the Butterfly Knife (2004)*
The Derrick Brown poetry collection that birthed Write Bloody Publishing.
Sincere, twisted, and violently romantic.

*I Love You Is Back (2006)*
A poetry collection by Derrick Brown.
"One moment tender, funny, or romantic, the next, visceral, ironic,
and revelatory—Here is the full chaos of life." (Janet Fitch, *White Oleander*)

*Scandalabra (2009)*
Former paratrooper Derrick Brown releases a stunning collection of poems written
at sea and in Nashville, TN. About.com's book of the year for poetry

*Don't Smell the Floss (2009)*
Award-winning writer Matty Byloos' first book of bizarre, absurd, and deliciously
perverse short stories puts your drunk uncle to shame.

*The Bones Below (2010)*
National Slam Champion Sierra DeMulder performs and teaches
with the release of her first book of hard-hitting, haunting poetry.

*The Constant Velocity of Trains (2008)*
The brain's left and right hemispheres collide in Lea Deschenes' Pushcart-Nominated
book of poetry about physics, relationships, and life's balancing acts.

*Heavy Lead Birdsong (2008)*
Award-winning academic poet Ryler Dustin releases his most
definitive collection of surreal love poetry.

*Uncontrolled Experiments in Freedom (2008)*
Boston underground art scene fixture Brian Ellis
becomes one of America's foremost narrative poetry performers.

*Ceremony for the Choking Ghost (2010)*
Slam legend Karen Finneyfrock's second book of poems ventures
into the humor and madness that surrounds familial loss.

*Pole Dancing to Gospel Hymns (2008)*
Andrea Gibson, a queer, award-winning poet who tours with Ani DiFranco,
releases a book of haunting, bold, nothing-but-the-truth ma'am poetry.

*City of Insomnia (2008)*
Victor D. Infante's noir-like exploration of unsentimental truth and poetic exorcism.

*The Last Time as We Are (2009)*
A new collection of poems from Taylor Mali, the author
of "What Teachers Make," the most forwarded poem in the world.

*In Search of Midnight: the Mike Mcgee Handbook of Awesome (2009)*
Slam's geek champion/class clown Mike McGee on his search for midnight
through hilarious prose, poetry, anecdotes, and how-to lists.

*Over the Anvil We Stretch (2008)*
2-time poetry slam champ Anis Mojgani's first collection: a Pushcart-Nominated
batch of backwood poetics, Southern myth, and rich imagery.

*Animal Ballistics (2009)*
Trading addiction and grief for empowerment and humor with her poetry,
Sarah Morgan does it best.

*Rise of the Trust Fall (2010)*
Award-winning feminist poet Mindy Nettifee
releases her second book of funny, daring, gorgeous, accessible poems.

*No More Poems About the Moon (2008)*
A pixilated, poetic and joyful view of a hyper-sexualized,
wholeheartedly confused, weird, and wild America with Michael Roberts.

*Miles of Hallelujah (2010)*
Slam poet/pop-culture enthusiast Rob "Ratpack Slim" Sturma
shows first collection of quirky, fantastic, romantic poetry.

*Spiking the Sucker Punch (2009)*
Nerd heartthrob, award-winning artist and performance poet,
Robbie Q. Telfer stabs your sensitive parts with his wit-dagger.

*Racing Hummingbirds (2010)*
Poet/performer Jeanann Verlee releases an award-winning book
of expertly crafted, startlingly honest, skin-kicking poems.

*Live for a Living (2007)*
Acclaimed performance poet Buddy Wakefield releases his second collection
about healing and charging into life face first.

# WRITE BLOODY ANTHOLOGIES

*The Elephant Engine High Dive Revival (2009)*
Our largest tour anthology ever! Features unpublished work by
Buddy Wakefield, Derrick Brown, Anis Mojgani and Shira Erlichman!

*The Good Things About America (2009)*
American poets team up with illustrators to recognize the beauty and wonder in our
nation. Various authors. Edited by Kevin Staniec and Derrick Brown

*Junkyard Ghost Revival (2008)*
Tour anthology of poets, teaming up for a journey of the US in a small van.
Heart-charging, socially active verse.

*The Last American Valentine:*
*Illustrated Poems To Seduce And Destroy (2008)*
Acclaimed authors including Jack Hirschman, Beau Sia, Jeffrey McDaniel,
Michael McClure, Mindy Nettifee and more. 24 authors and 12 illustrators
team up for a collection of non-sappy love poetry. Edited by Derrick Brown

*Learn Then Burn (2010)*
Exciting classroom-ready anthology for introducing new writers
to the powerful world of poetry. Edited by Tim Stafford and Derrick Brown.

*Learn Then Burn Teacher's Manual (2010)*
Turn key classroom-safe guide Tim Stafford and Molly Meacham
to accompany *Learn Then Burn*: A modern poetry anthology for the classroom.

**WWW.WRITEBLOODY.COM**

**WRITEBLOODY**
QUALITY AMERICAN BOOKS

## PULL YOUR BOOKS UP
## BY THEIR BOOTSTRAPS

Write Bloody Publishing distributes and promotes great books of fiction, poetry and art every year. We are an independent press dedicated to quality literature and book design, with an office in Long Beach, CA.

Our employees are authors and artists so we call ourselves a family. Our design team comes from all over America: modern painters, photographers and rock album designers create book covers we're proud to be judged by.

We publish and promote 8-12 tour-savvy authors per year. We are grass-roots, D.I.Y., bootstrap believers. Pull up a good book and join the family. Support independent authors, artists and presses.

Visit us online:

**WRITEBLOODY.COM**

CPSIA information can be obtained
at www.ICGtesting.com
Printed in the USA
FSOW01n0448120716
22607FS